White-Tailed Deer

I0146146

Victoria Blakemore

For Mom, for always being there for me.

© 2017 Victoria Blakemore

All rights reserved. This book or parts thereof may not be reproduced in any form, stored in any retrieval system, or transmitted in any form by any means—electronic, mechanical, photocopy, recording, or otherwise—without   prior written permission of the publisher, except as provided by United States of America copyright law. For permission requests, write to the publisher, at "Attention: Permissions Coordinator," at the address below.

vblakemore.author@gmail.com

Copyright info/picture credits

Cover, kmm7553/AdobeStock; Page 3, rayhennessy/AdobeStock; Page 5, Tony Campbell/AdobeStock; Page 7, diane616/Pixabay; Page 9, GIS/Adobestock; Pages 10-11, CCat82/AdobeStock; Page 13, jimcumming88/Adobestock; Page 15, bones64/Pixabay; Page 17, Ron Rowan/AdobeStock; Page 19, Steve Oehlenschlager/AdobeStock; Page 21, kmm7553/AdobeStock; Page 23; edbo23/Pixabay; Page 25, smarko/Pixabay; Page 27, diane616/Pixabay; Page 29, WikimediaImages/Pixabay; Page 31, brm1949/AdobeStock; Page 33, Stephen Finn/AdobeStock

Table of Contents

What Are White-Tailed Deer?

White-tailed deer are mammals. They are the smallest members of the North American deer family.

They are tan or brown in the summer and more of a gray-brown in the winter.

The color of their fur helps

them to blend in to their

surroundings.

Size

White-tailed deer can be up to about seven feet long. They may stand as tall as six feet with their antlers.

Males may weigh up to 300 pounds. Females are smaller and may weigh up to 200 pounds.

Physical Characteristics

White-tailed deer get their name from the white fur that they have under their tail. It can be used as a warning signal if there is danger nearby.

Their eyes are located on the sides of their head. They can see on both sides of their body.

White-tailed deer have large ears and a good sense of hearing. They are able to hear **predators** from far away.

Habitat

White-tailed deer are found in the forests and wooded areas. They can also be seen **grazing** in fields.

In many places, white-tailed deer live close to humans and may be seen in gardens and backyards.

Range

White-tailed deer are found in most parts of the United States and southern Canada.

They are not found in Alaska, Hawaii, and parts of the Southwest.

Diet

White-tailed deer are **herbivores**, which means that they eat only plants.

Their diet is made up of leaves, twigs, lichen, grass, fruits, nuts, and corn.

White-tailed deer tend to graze

early in the morning and late in

the afternoon.

They have a stomach that is like a cow's stomach. It has special **chambers** that help it to digest plants.

The chambers break down the food, remove the extra water, and absorb the **nutrients**.

In the winter, food is **scarce**.

White-tailed deer eat buds

and twigs because there isn't

much else for them to eat.

Communication

White-tailed deer use sound,
scent, and movement to
communicate with each other.

They flash the white fur of their
tail to warn other deer if there
is danger nearby. They may
also snort or bleat as a
warning.

White-tailed deer mark their

trail as they walk with special

scent glands on their feet. 17

Movement

White-tailed deer are very fast and have been known to run up to 30 miles per hour.

They have strong legs and are able to jump as high as ten feet.

White-tailed deer are able
to leap as far as thirty feet in
a single jump.

Bucks

Male white-tailed deer are called bucks. They have antlers that they shed and regrow each year.

Older deer have antlers that are larger and have more points.

Bucks may fight other bucks

with their antlers to defend

their **territory**.

Does

Female white-tailed deer are called does. They do not have antlers.

Does are very protective of their babies. When they need to look for food, they leave their babies in a hiding spot in tall grass until they come back.

Does usually have their babies in

the springtime.

23

Fawns

White-tailed deer usually have between one and three babies. Their babies are called fawns.

When they are first born, fawns have white spots. Their spots help them to blend in so that they are safe from predators.

Fawns stay with their mothers
for between one and two
years.

Life Span

White-tailed deer have been known to live as long as twenty years, but most live less than ten years in the wild.

Predators such as bobcats, wolves, and coyotes hunt white-tailed deer for food.

Population

White-tailed deer populations can grow very quickly.

In some places, populations can get too big for the environment. If this happens, there is not enough food for deer and they may starve.

Deer hunting helps to control deer populations in some areas of the United States.

Helping White-Tailed Deer

Finding food in the winter can be hard for deer. Twigs and buds are usually the only food available.

Some people put out food such as dried corn in the woods and fields. This provides extra food for the deer.

Cars can be very dangerous for deer. They may need to cross roads to find food, which puts them at risk of getting hit by cars.

Deer crossing signs help to warn drivers that deer may be crossing the road.

Glossary

Chamber: a compartment

Grazing: feeding on growing

grass and plants

Herbivore: an animal that eats

only plants

Nutrients: things in food that help

plants, animals, and people to

grow

Predator: an animal that hunts

other animals for food

Scarce: hard to find, not much

left

Territory: an area of land that an

animal claims as its own

About the Author

Victoria Blakemore is a first grade

teacher in Southwest Florida with a

passion for reading.

You can visit her at

www.enchantedinelementary.com

Also in This Series

Elementary Explorers **Gray Wolves** Victoria Blakemore	Elementary Explorers **Sloths** Victoria Blakemore	Elementary Explorers **Flamingos** Victoria Blakemore	Elementary Explorers **Camels** Victoria Blakemore	Elementary Explorers **Koalas** Victoria Blakemore	Elementary Explorers **Honey Bees** Victoria Blakemore
Elementary Explorers **Pandas** Victoria Blakemore	Elementary Explorers **Pangolins** Victoria Blakemore	Elementary Explorers **White-Tailed Deer** Victoria Blakemore	Elementary Explorers **Orcas** Victoria Blakemore	Elementary Explorers **Giraffes** Victoria Blakemore	Elementary Explorers **Corn** Victoria Blakemore
Elementary Explorers **Meerkats** Victoria Blakemore	Elementary Explorers **Echidnas** Victoria Blakemore	Elementary Explorers **Walruses** Victoria Blakemore	Elementary Explorers **Raccoons** Victoria Blakemore	Elementary Explorers **Bald Eagles** Victoria Blakemore	Elementary Explorers **Apples** Victoria Blakemore
Elementary Explorers **Arctic Foxes** Victoria Blakemore	Elementary Explorers **Red Pandas** Victoria Blakemore	Elementary Explorers **Cassowaries** Victoria Blakemore	Elementary Explorers **Tigers** Victoria Blakemore	Elementary Explorers **Ladybugs** Victoria Blakemore	Elementary Explorers **Moose** Victoria Blakemore
Elementary Explorers **Beluga Whales** Victoria Blakemore	Elementary Explorers **Leopards** Victoria Blakemore	Elementary Explorers **Elephants** Victoria Blakemore	Elementary Explorers **Jellyfish** Victoria Blakemore	Elementary Explorers **Binturongs** Victoria Blakemore	Elementary Explorers **Lions** Victoria Blakemore
Elementary Explorers **Dolphins** Victoria Blakemore	Elementary Explorers **Reindeer** Victoria Blakemore	Elementary Explorers **Hammerhead Sharks** Victoria Blakemore	Elementary Explorers **Hippos** Victoria Blakemore	Elementary Explorers **Pumpkins** Victoria Blakemore	Elementary Explorers **Peafowl** Victoria Blakemore

Also in This Series

Elementary Explorers — **Chameleons** — Victoria Blakemore

Elementary Explorers — **Florida Panthers** — Victoria Blakemore

Elementary Explorers — **Aye-Ayes** — Victoria Blakemore

Elementary Explorers — **Black Bears** — Victoria Blakemore

Elementary Explorers — **Cheetahs** — Victoria Blakemore

Elementary Explorers — **Manatees** — Victoria Blakemore

Elementary Explorers — **Gingerbread** — Victoria Blakemore

Elementary Explorers — **Polar Bears** — Victoria Blakemore

Elementary Explorers — **Hot Chocolate** — Victoria Blakemore

Elementary Explorers — **Orangutans** — Victoria Blakemore

Elementary Explorers — **Coyotes** — Victoria Blakemore

Elementary Explorers — **Marshmallows** — Victoria Blakemore

Elementary Explorers — **Strawberries** — Victoria Blakemore

Elementary Explorers — **Aardvarks** — Victoria Blakemore

Elementary Explorers — **Mako Sharks** — Victoria Blakemore

Elementary Explorers — **Alligators** — Victoria Blakemore

Elementary Explorers — **Frogs** — Victoria Blakemore

www.ingramcontent.com/pod-product-compliance
Lightning Source LLC
Chambersburg PA
CBHW040347050426
42336CB00056B/3390

9 780999 985572